First published in the United States in 1988 by Oxford University Press, Inc.,
200 Madison Avenue, New York, New York 1001

Published in Great Britain in 1987 by Methuen Children's Books Ltd., London

Text copyright © 1987 by Graeme Garden   *17.69*
Illustrations copyright © 1987 by Neil Canning

Oxford is a registered trademark of Oxford University Press

Library of Congress Cataloging-in-Publication Data

Garden, Graeme.
   The Skylighters.

   Summary: A collection of poems trace the activities
of a shadowy little band of characters that secretly
creates our skyscapes, painting sunsets, clouds, rain,
and fog.
   1. Sky – Juvenile poetry.   2. Children's poetry,
English. [1. Sky – Poetry.   2. English poetry]
I. Canning, Neil, ill.   II. Title.
PR6057.A625S58 1988   821'.914   87-31304
ISBN 0-19-520642-8

Printed in Hong Kong
by South China Printing Co

The Skylighters

Graeme Garden *and* Neil Canning

OXFORD UNIVERSITY PRESS
New York

Skylighters

You know there are Skylighters, lighting the sky?
Oh, there are. Just look up, right up there, very high,
And you'll see all their paint and their color and dye –
But you won't see the Skylighters lighting the sky.

Old Mr Blue

His real name is Grandfather Jonathan Cotton,
(The Master of Color and Hue),
Which all of the Skylighters must have forgotten;
To them he's just 'Old Mr Blue'!

He mixes the sky-wash, beginning at midnight,
And works through the dark at his art.
Until he announces the colors are mixed right,
The morning quite simply can't start.

The blues that he chooses to use for the day may be
Indigo, Cobalt, or Green,
Forget-me-not, Royal, or Peacock, or Navy,
Or Prussian, or Ultramarine.

In winter it's cold and he can't work so quickly
Preparing his Blue for the morn.
But summer is hot, so he mixes more slickly –
By four he delivers the Dawn.

Day Colors

See! Teetering, tottering, high as they dare,
The Skywash Brigade are at work in the air.
All bobbing and wobbling, hanging on tight,
Until the bright Day Colors cover the night.

"Hey, watch out there! Oops! Hang On! Careful with that!"
It's hard work and dangerous ("Hold on to your hat!").
When Morning Cloud coloring's done they all vote
To nip home for breakfast, and skip the third coat.

Sky Paint

Dandy Dan De Dolamore
Is captain of the color store.
Darkest black or hint of white
He'll get the tint of the sky light right.

Cadmium yellow: for a mid-day sun that's mellow.
Pale grey : for an autumn day.
Coral pink : which is used more often than you think.
Lilac : which you'll never see a dawn sky lack.
Prussian blue : a popular evening hue.
Chinese white : not required at night.
Vermilion : a hue in a trillion.
Magenta : handy for a rainbow center.
Lime green : for a streak in a sunset seldom seen.
Crimson : for the edges of dark clouds with red rims on.
And so on,
And so on.

(Dan's assistant, Master Strong,
Sometimes gets the colors wrong.)

Mackerel Sky

The sky light is pale, but it's luminous too,
With a rhythm that drums on the eye.
The cloud-scattered pattern is dusky and blue,
And they call it the Mackerel Sky.

They dash on the strokes, why their sky-brushes fly!
So the colors are fresh, bright and new;
They must have the steadiest hand, heart and eye,
The brave boys of the Mackerel Crew.

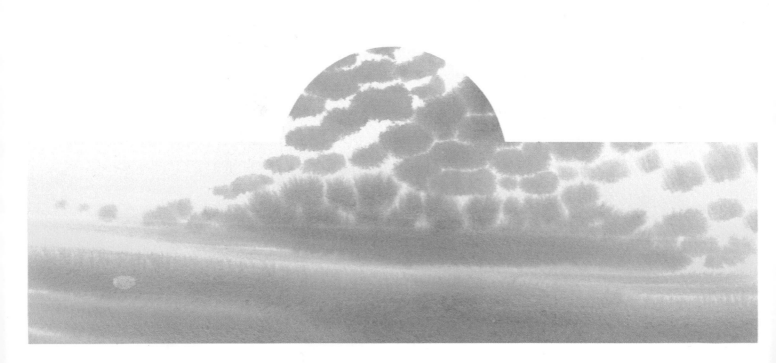

Cloud-hammer

Young Rosie McPherson-McPhail
Has a cloud-hammer, bought in a sale;
She'll tap on a cloud
Which explodes (very loud)
And the bits clatter downwards as hail.

Wet Sky

The sky is dry, so crisp and clear,
And Skylighters have fun.
But when the rain and sleet appear
The colors smudge and run.

Lightning

When brewing up a symphony
Of sky-lit electricity,
An orchestra of engineers
(Protected eyes and padded ears),
Each one working at his station
(Rubber gloves for insulation),
All obey their sole instructor –
He's the

FLASH

Lightning Conductor

Fog Blind

When autumn sun deserts the sky,
  the world grows grim and grisly.
The dying leaves droop on the twig,
  the air is dim and drizzly.
The Skylighters paint dull and grey
  a sky that seems to frown,
And so, on this unhappy scene,
  they pull the Fog Blind down.

The Sunset Pots

As twilight falls the fading sun
　　is winched down in the west;
And this, of all the times of day,
　　the Skylighters love best.
They open up the Sunset Pots
　　and madly rush about
Slapping the colors on the sky . . .
　　until the paint runs out.

Moon Gang

Cut, riveted, welded, and polished so bright,
The Full Moon is hauled aloft into the night.
The Moon-Gang at last take a tea-break, and then
Begin the month's Moon-work all over again.

Each day, very carefully, they trim off a slice,
(The slices they cut are extremely precise)
Those nice precise slices are gathered, for soon
They'll be melted and beaten to make the next moon.

The pay for the day is so little you'd laugh,
(Full pay for a full Moon, half pay for a half).
O'Gorman the Foreman, if asked, will reply:
"The Moon is a very small part of the sky."

"It may well be small," cries old Phoebe McFly,
"But at night-time the Moon catches everyone's eye;
So pay us our dues, or we'll show you the door, man,
You Norman O'Gorman, for all you're the Foreman."

Night Sky

Look up in the night at the sky, dark and deep,
And you'll see what the Night-Lighters do while we sleep.
Where's Pluto? Where's Mercury, Venus, or Mars?
They pin-point the planets, and sort out the stars.

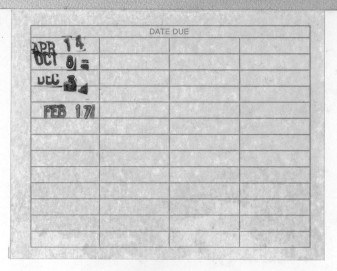